OUR BAD MAGNET

Douglas Maxwell

OUR BAD MAGNET

OBERON BOOKS
LONDON

WWW.OBERONBOOKS.COM

First published in 2001 by Oberon Books Ltd.
521 Caledonian Road, London N7 9RH
Tel: +44 (0) 20 7607 3637 / Fax: +44 (0) 20 7607 3629
e-mail: info@oberonbooks.com
www.oberonbooks.com

A catalogue record for this book is available from the British
Library.

PB ISBN: 9781840022445
E ISBN: 9781849438643

Cover photography by Kevin Low

Visit www.oberonbooks.com to read more about all our books
and to buy them. You will also find features, author interviews and
news of any author events, and you can sign up for e-newsletters
so that you're always first to hear about our new releases.

Author's Note

We are in Girvan. A small town on the south west coast of Scotland. A small, dead seaside place. It used to be a popular holiday resort for Glasgow in it's heyday – not any more. Amusements and paddle boats just sit there empty. Casuals gather on the corners. Shops get boarded up every now and then. Big enough to have a couple of nice neighbourhoods and a newspaper for the area, but small enough for everyone to know everyone else.

There are two sections to the stage. To the rear of stage right is a large ramp leading to an acting area perhaps 5ft off the ground. The ramp has a dramatic drop and for the bulk of the play is used a cliff face. The rest of the stage can be used in its entirety. To the rear of stage left is a large machine covered in tarpaulin with a tube which disappears up into the lights. More of this strange device later.

The play exists in two 'states'. The first is the real world. This is the natural turning of events. Even when the play goes back to their child and teenage stories, it should be presented as realistic and easy going. The second is the story world. Whenever a story is told a significant stylistic change should occur on stage. Whoever is narrating the story will address the audience and the actors play all the extra characters mentioned as the narrative goes along.

Hand for the bands.
Thanks to Salvador, The Girlfriends
and The Dug James Singers.

Characters

ALAN
At age 9, 19 and 29

FRASER
At age 9, 19 and 29

PAUL
At age 9, 19 and 29

GORDON (Giggles)
At age 9 and 19

Our Bad Magnet was first performed at the Tron Theatre, Glasgow on 1 July 2000, with the following cast:

ALAN, Barrie Hunter

FRASER, Steven Duffy

PAUL, Gary McInnes

GIGGLES, Alasdair Macrae

Director, Jim Twaddale

Designer, Alan Reid

Costume Designer, Marion Thomson

Lighting Designer, Fleur Woolford

ACT ONE

Lights up on the ramp. Or, lights up on the cliff just over the Horse Rocks. These are not cliffs in the dramatic, sheer face, edge of a continent sense – more like a small hill with a bit missing. The sea is below, but not far below. The town of Girvan is five minutes back the other way.

Enter ALAN (29) up the ramp. He is cocooned inside a massive waterproof jacket – the type football managers or car salesmen wear. Beneath this outer skin is a short-sleeved shirt and a particularly nasty tie; grey trousers that don't belong to a suit and scuffed 'good shoes'. He checks the view and lets out a big 'Aaaahhh', the type usually reserved for after large meals. Big smile. He loves this. Doesn't really know what to do so he sits on the edge and lets his feet dangle over the side. He sits like an adult, making sure there's no muck on his trousers and that no one can see him struggling to get comfortable. Another big 'Aaaahhh!', this time it's pronounced 'No honestly, I'm really enjoying this'.

Enter FRASER (29) from stage left on ground level. FRASER has the look and scowl of a student. A long, second hand coat pulled up around him like an arctic explorer. Everything ALAN loves about this place FRASER hates. He looks awkward, lost and pissed off. ALAN has seen him. ALAN shouts 'HO!' and gives a big wave. FRASER waves back unsure of who it is. Then he makes him out. They are obviously too far away from each other to speak, so they communicate in waves. ALAN waves for FRASER to come up to the cliff. FRASER waves 'why don't you come down here?' ALAN waves 'No, you come up here'. FRASER exits the way he came in a cloud of mutters and head shaking. ALAN laughs and stands up looking for FRASER's approach. ALAN obviously sees him coming up the hill and starts to shout to the back of the stage. It's all in an overly familiar joke tone.

ALAN: And you join us here on the last day of the Girvan international mountaineering championships. And here's last year's winner, Fraser Hamilton struggling up the perilous north face of the Horse Rocks. Huffing and puffing like an old bas...OH!!! He's fallen. Ha ha ha ha he's fallen. Slipped in something unpleasant. Ha ha ha !!! The kids on the swings behind him are loving this.

The rest of the time between now and FRASER's entrance up the ramp is taken up with ALAN laughing. When he does appear FRASER's whole right hand side is covered in dirt, he's a little out of breath and is only just managing to keep a hold on his dislike for everything he sees.

Hey! Here he is! Here he is! Who's this mysterious stranger covered in cack? Eh? Who is it? I know that face.

FRASER: (*Nowhere near smiling. Tolerating.*) All right?

ALAN: I know that face. A blast from the past. Can't remember the name though.

FRASER: How you doing Alan? You all right?

ALAN: Oh yes it's all coming back now. Distant memories. Is it...is...Fraser? Is that right? Am I on the right track? Is it Fraser Bamilton? No...Damilton? No Fraser Hamilton, that's it! Fraser Hamilton the one and only. Ha ha ha aaaaah.

A nodding pause.

FRASER: So you all right?

ALAN: (*Shakes his head.*) You're no getting away that easy pal. C'mere.

FRASER: What?

ALAN: I haven't seen you in a million years, now c'mere.

FRASER: Where?

ALAN: Here. You're getting a hug big man. No arguments.

FRASER: Oh for f...

ALAN grips FRASER's whole body in a powerful, joy-ous hug. FRASER's arms are pinned against his own chest. Finally released.

ALAN: How you doing? How you doing? You look great. It's great to see you. Brilliant. Oh this is brilliant.

FRASER: How are you? You look…very successful.

ALAN: Ducking and diving. Tina says Hi.

FRASER: Right.

ALAN: It's great you could come. When'd you get in?

FRASER: Just there. So…

ALAN: So…

FRASER: So…what's this incredible news Paul was on about? And when do I get to say I told you all along?

ALAN: It's a wee surprise.

FRASER: Is this where we're going to do it? The cliffs?

ALAN: Well no. I thought we could go back to the scene of the crime. As I say, I've got a wee surprise for you both. I've been building it in the hut.

FRASER: Building it? What do you mean, I thought…

ALAN: Ah ah ah…it's a surprise. I didn't think you'd come actually.

FRASER: Well…I wasn't going to until Paul said there was this amazing revelation, but I'm beginning to think I've got the wrong end of the stick.

ALAN: (*Oblivious.*) I was saying to Tina, it's ten years on, you know. We should do something between the three of us to remember. Just between us. Keep it going. That's when I came up with the idea of the machine.

FRASER: The machine? What's going on here? What about…?

ALAN: Oop. Said too much. Don't want to spoil it. Name, rank and number. Ha ha ha.

FRASER: God. (*Looks over the edge.*)

ALAN: Yeah it's great isn't it? I thought this would be a nice place to meet. This was where we first got to know him and that.

FRASER: (*Getting frustrated.*) Alan… (*In a lighter tone.*) Doesn't it do your nut in living here?

ALAN: (*Well rehearsed.*) Well to be perfectly honest with you Fraser, when we first got married we talked about Glasgow and at one time even Ayr, but there were pros and cons. It's good for kids – the sea's there and the park and so on. We've got a nice house in Miller Avenue and there's my work which is Ayrshire based.

FRASER: What is it you do again? Engineer?

ALAN: Civil engineer aye. I'm actually on a site just out of town at the moment. You know out at the golf course? There. Part of the strategy redevelopment for the 2000 project. I'm the consultant for Scottish Enterprise. The middle man. Stop the client and the contractor fighting. Ha ha ha. Try and keep everyone happy. I love it. Bit of travelling but it's good. I was in Cumnock last week. It's all about communication. (*Excited.*) Oh by the way I've got some news for you about our words. I'll tell you later though. Aye, it's all about communication. Make sure each part of the team knows where they stand vis-à-vis the overall strategy.

FRASER: But how…what do you do here? There's nothing to do. Literally.

ALAN: No no no. Plenty. Pubs, putting…and don't forget the Vikings.

FRASER: 'Don't forget the Vikings'?

ALAN: The Viking Society. I'm a member.

FRASER: You're a member of the Vikings?

ALAN: Brilliant. You should think about it. It's basically a good excuse for a few beers and days out in Largs. We all get the kit on, re-enact a few battles, make some jewellery, build a fire and get steaming. Ace. You should come. We're off to York next weekend. You don't have to wear kit. Get the beers down you. Brilliant.

FRASER: Do you do much raping and pillaging?

ALAN: Ha ha, no.

FRASER: If there was a society for that I'd join. Kit or no kit.

ALAN: You'd like it. Your mum says you're still in Glasgow?

FRASER: Well… Thinking about London.

ALAN: What you doing for work?

FRASER: This and that.

Pause.

ALAN: Are you going to pop in on your mum and dad, seeing as you're in town?

FRASER: I suppose so. I'm not staying though. After we get this over with I'm away up the road. Don't want to spend any more time with them than I have to.

ALAN: Well you know what they say; you can choose your friends, but you can't choose your family.

FRASER: I never chose my friends.

ALAN: Ha ha, no I suppose not. Daft saying. (*Looking off.*) Oh…

Pause. ALAN's spotted someone coming up the hill.

(*Shouting off.*) You join us here on the last day of the Girvan international mountaineering championship and here comes last year's champion, Mr Paul Lassels!

Again, a great deal of laughing greets the entrance of PAUL (29). He is wearing an expensive looking suit and a tailored coat. He has a wave of well looked-after hair and a grin of white teeth. He carries a leather attaché case. Big strides, firm handshakes. He's laughing all the way with ALAN's patented mountaineering gag.

PAUL: Hello!!! The boys. The boys are here. Mountaineering champion, what're you like?

ALAN: Here he is the very man. Just talking about you.

PAUL: I'll deny everything in court!

Big laughs from PAUL and ALAN.

ALAN: How? What have you been up to? Ha ha ha…

PAUL: Nothing you wouldn't do mate! Ha ha ha…know what I mean? Fraser.

FRASER: Paul.

PAUL: Nice of you to make it mate. I know you're busy. But Alan and I have some great news about the manuscripts, at last. And has he (*ALAN.*) told you about the news about his word?

ALAN: If you don't mind Paul, I'd like to keep that till the meeting.

PAUL: Oh fair enough chief. You're the boss.

ALAN: (*To PAUL.*) Have you brought the proofs?

FRASER: Proofs?

PAUL: The book. We finally got a publisher. After all these years man.

FRASER: I thought you did all that. Published the stories and everything?

PAUL: Oh that's small potatoes. This is the real deal baby. Big bucks. Never mind that, we'll go over that later. How you doing my man? You've been missing in action for a few years.

FRASER: Oh…ups and downs.

PAUL: Married or…?

FRASER: No.

PAUL: Me neither. It's only fat boy here that's been snared. He's a Viking now was he telling you? Have you ever heard anything as ridiculous in all your life?

ALAN: You're just jealous.

PAUL: Jealous? Of a bunch a grown men sitting round a fire with horns on their heads, drinking mead and talking about Star Trek?

ALAN: We don't wear horns. That's a myth.

PAUL: That's a cry for help boss, that's what that is.

ALAN and PAUL laugh, good mates. FRASER forces a smile which looks very much like a grimace.

FRASER: So I take it you two are in contact with each other these days?

PAUL: In contact? You make it sound like military manoeuvres. Aye, well we do speak on the phone when there's a story getting published. Do you get the cheques by the way?

FRASER: Yeah. Thanks.

ALAN: Paul's office is in London. We met up when me and Tina went down for a winter break. He took us to lunch. And very nice it was too.

PAUL: Not at all mate. Happy to do it. Wish I saw more of you. (*To FRASER.*) And you sir! Don't think you're just going to mosey into the sunset and disappear for another three years.

ALAN: Shall we go down to the wee school and get things started?

FRASER: The wee school! We're not doing it in there!

ALAN: It's all right. David Nicholl's the janitor there. We don't have to break a window this time. They rebuilt it. It's a community centre now. They linedance in there.

FRASER: It's not that. It's just…I don't know if I could go back. I've no been back to the wee school since. Can we not go somewhere a bit more decent?

PAUL: Young engineer of the year here has built a machine he wants us to see. He's been in the hut for a month Tina says.

FRASER: I cannae do this.

PAUL: Don't ruin it, it can't hurt to…

FRASER: I'm not ruining anything. I never wanted to do this in the first place. I think it's daft. We should just forget all about it.

ALAN: Forget all about it? Looks like you've already forgotten all about it.

FRASER: Don't tell me what I feel, ya nimston! You don't have a clue. You've been stuck in a rut for the last five years in this dump. This is probably the first exciting thing you've done since your last Viking raid.

ALAN: All I'm saying is…

FRASER: Probably been looking forward to this…

PAUL: Right!! Shut it. Okay pals here's the deal. We made a promise and we made a bet. Tonight we put an end to both. After tonight we don't have to lay eyes on each other ever again. Lets put this tiff down to excitement shall we? Mates?

ALAN: (*Immediately.*) I'm really sorry Fraser. It's been a hard day for me. Contractors cutting costs in one ear, landscape designers adding costs in the other. I was taking it out on you.

ALAN holds his hands out to shake. FRASER accepts.

FRASER: Sorry.

ALAN: Sorry mate. C'mere.

FRASER: Oh no, for Christ sake.

Another hug from ALAN. It's so gratuitous that it forces a laugh out of FRASER.

PAUL: Okay lovebirds, save the bumming till after I'm away. Let's get this over with.

ALAN: Oh hang on. I want to cover up the machine. I'll set it off at the end of the meeting. Walk slow. I'll see you in there. (*Exit ALAN happily.*)

PAUL: (*To FRASER.*) As Han Solo would say, 'I'm getting a bad feeling about this'. It's good of you to come back for this.

FRASER: To be honest, I think I'm here under false pretences. For some reason I thought you had some big news.

PAUL: We do.

FRASER: I thought...you had bigger news than whatever Alan's built in his hut.

PAUL: How do you mean?

FRASER: I dunno. I suppose I thought that...

PAUL: Fraser mate, you don't still believe all that do you? After all these years?

FRASER shrugs and smiles. They walk off down the hill. There is a pause. We're going back. Enter FRASER, PAUL, ALAN and GIGGLES, all aged nine, up the ramp. They have their school bags with them. They're on their way home. FRASER is in a new looking school uniform, the rest are just in school stuff, no ties but quite smart, or they would be if the shirts were tucked in and their faces weren't mucky. ALAN is officially fat. He loses the weight with time, but not the comments. The order of command is FRASER – the leader, all talk and orders, then PAUL. PAUL more or less idolises FRASER and is second in command. They both out rank ALAN by a long way. He tags along because he lives near here. He is pretending to be thicker than he actually is in an unusual attempt to be liked and make the others laugh. GIGGLES is new to the school. He is a dour, dour boy. He doesn't smile – ever. When he talks it is with slow deliberation. Sadness is his uniform, even at nine years old. They throw down their bags and perch on the edge. ALAN collapses on the grass. GIGGLES stands just to the side, unsure what to do.

FRASER: Who's got a pencil and paper then?

PAUL: Me.

ALAN: I can't breathe man.

FRASER: Shouldnae be so fat.

PAUL: Fatboy.

ALAN: (*To PAUL.*) Shut it you!

PAUL: Or what?

ALAN: Fraser? Sure me and you had a hefty time the day? On that message to the big school? What a laugh man.

PAUL: So? I've been to the big school millions of times.

FRASER: Pencil!

ALAN and PAUL have a short race to see who can get the pencil first. PAUL wins and gives ALAN a huge grin. In retaliation ALAN gives GIGGLES a 'What are you looking at' face.

Right quit it yous. Let's write the words down so we know who's got what.

ALAN: What are we doing again?

PAUL: Spazzy! We were talking about it all the way up the road.

ALAN: I couldnae hear you I was behind.

PAUL: Stuffing Space Raiders in your fat face.

ALAN: No I wasnae.

FRASER: Shut up ya dick. Right man, what we're doing right, is making up words.

ALAN: Aw right. How?

PAUL: 'Cause of this guy Fraser knows.

FRASER: I don't know him, he's dead.

ALAN: Who?

FRASER: This guy. He wrote stories. I saw this thing last night right? It was on Blue Peter...

ALAN: Aw naw! You don't watch Blue Peter man! ha ha ha

FRASER: And it said he made up words. Made them up man. If he couldnae think of a word he made them up. And guess what? They turned into proper words. I can't remember them now but we use them, every day!

ALAN: So? I make up stuff all the time.

FRASER: Aye but other folk don't use your words but.

ALAN: Aye but...

PAUL: Shut up Alan.

FRASER: So I says to Paul that we should have a game. It'll be a hefty laugh. And we can bet on it.

This pulls them in closer.

ALAN: A bet! Yeees.

FRASER: We all write down a word – a new word! – and whoever gets that word into the dictionary first wins a fiver. Imagine it. Something that one of us make up, being used all over the world forever and ever. It would be amazing.

ALAN: Who's going to give us the fiver?

FRASER: I'll get my dad to give us it.

PAUL: Won't it take ages though? To get a word in the dictionary. Fraser, won't it take ages?

FRASER: Aye. It'll take about…a year.

ALAN: A year! I need that fiver now but.

PAUL: Who says your word will get in the dictionary?

ALAN: Me.

FRASER: Hefty. Right Paul, what's your word?

FRASER is taking notes.

ALAN: Wait! Is Giggles in this?

FRASER: I dunno. Giggles, you in this? You can be if you want?

GIGGLES: Okay.

GIGGLES sits down just outside their circle. PAUL tries to get FRASER to rethink this decision with a series of nods and grimaces.

ALAN: Don't duff this up Giggles, I got you in, remember that.

FRASER: Go Paul.

PAUL: Em…what was it… Nimston. My word was Nimston. N-i-m-s…n-i-m-s, N-I-M-S-T-O-N.

FRASER: Right. What's it mean?

PAUL: Eh, it's someone with one leg.

This causes absolute hilarity in ALAN. He rolls about.

ALAN: Ha ha ha one leg! No way! One leg! How can someone have one leg?

PAUL: How can they no?

ALAN: Ye cannae get one leg.

PAUL: Don't be such a fanny, of course you can. Tommy Hughes's dad's got one leg.

FRASER: He's right. Tommy's dad's a *total* nimston.

ALAN: He's got two legs.

PAUL: Aye one's wooden but!

ALAN: So he's got two. One normal, one wood. Two.

FRASER: Nimston means one real leg Alan. Stop ruining it.

ALAN: (*Sulking a bit.*) I hate nimstons man.

PAUL: (*Still to ALAN.*) You got a word?

ALAN: Aye! (*Gets up and looks about for inspiration.*) Eh…my word is…eh…

PAUL: He doesnae have a word.

ALAN: I do! And it's miles better than your word. Eh…

PAUL: Guess what colour Alan's on in SRA? Aqua. Ha ha ha.

ALAN: So? Eh…

FRASER: Hurry up!

ALAN: My word is… Crack…cracka…crackakola… crackacookoo! Crackacookoo. That's it.

FRASER: How do you spell it?

ALAN: I dunno. Guess what it means. (*Still trying to figure that out himself.*) It means… (*Sees the swings in the distance.*) you know when you try to bronco a swing but you get it wrong and it scons you on the face and you start greetin'? That's a crackacookoo. That fiver's mine man. Ha ha ha.

PAUL: That must mean you're a crackacookoo.

ALAN: Naw!

FRASER: What if a nimston's on a swing and tries to bronco?

PAUL: (*Matter of fact.*) Nimstons shouldnae be on swings.

ALAN: Aye but they can be. Then they are a cracka-cookoonimston.

FRASER: Okay. My word is…toom. T-O-O-M. It means a place like this where you can see everything. You know how up here you can see from the station and the churches and the main street and the harbour and all the houses an that? And this way, you get the scheme and the sea and hills. This place is a toom place. But a toom place has to have…eh…a bit like this right? A bit that if you jump off you die.

ALAN: 'Member that time I jumped off the pier?

PAUL: You never jumped off the pier.

ALAN: Aye I did.

PAUL: You fell off the pier.

ALAN: Same difference.

PAUL: Fell off the pier onto a boat.

ALAN: It's more than you've ever done.

PAUL: Shut it man, I've fallen out a car when it's been totally going.

ALAN: I'm a spazzy! (*Complete with gestures.*)

FRASER: Giggles. You next.

GIGGLES: I don't think I can.

FRASER: How?

PAUL: If he cannae do it just leave him out of it. It was our idea anyway.

FRASER: If fat Alan can do it you can do it.

GIGGLES: No thanks.

ALAN: I thought you were meant to be special?

PAUL & FRASER: Ssshh, ya dick, shut it, etc.

GIGGLES: What?

ALAN: Nothing. Well, it's just that the day before you came to school Mrs Grey told us that you were a special case or something and, like, we weren't to mention it.

PAUL and FRASER shake their heads at ALAN's insensitivity.

PAUL: It wasnae that.

ALAN: Aye it was. She said you were special and even though you were quiet, you were really clever. And that's why she made Fraser be pals with you because he's the cleverest boy in the class. She said you write wee stories and one had won a competition. But you had taken a total spazzy attack at your last school and that's how you came here. She said that we'd not to mention that we knew about the spazzy attack or the stories. So we never.

FRASER: If you can write stories, you can make up words. Imagine it, even after you die people will still be using your word. And the first one to do it wins a fiver. So come on then. Come on Giggles give us a word.

GIGGLES: I...can't.

FRASER: Oh well. Your loss.

ALAN: How come you don't ever smile Giggles? You've been in our class for about three days and you've no smiled once? You didnae even smile when Anne Marie eat all that butter.

GIGGLES: I don't know.

ALAN: Is it because you're a wee spazzy? A special spazzy? You can get them.

GIGGLES: I'm not a spazzy.

FRASER: I write stories as well. We all do. On Friday afternoons after 'Word Perfect Spelling'. What was that story I wrote once about Face from the A Team, 'member?

PAUL: Yeah, it was ace…

GIGGLES is now distracting PAUL and ALAN from FRASER.

How come you don't smile?

GIGGLES: I don't know. I'm not that happy.

ALAN: What ever?

GIGGLES: Not really.

ALAN: Mind you I hate school. I really hate school. 'Member that time I chucked that stone at wee Mitchell and it went flying by him and smashed Mrs Thompson's car window? I totally bombed it right? I hid in Shanty Shaws. Mitchell told me that Mrs Thompson knew it was me that done it! But it was a Friday right? So I had to wait all weekend before I got into trouble. I never smiled once all Saturday and all Sunday. My guts were totally going mental. I hate Mitchell do you?

PAUL: When I'm bad and I get shouted at I just watch TV. That always cheers me up. Airwolf, Knightrider, Streethawk, Blue Thunder. Anything that's got a crime-fighting machine that can talk. I cheer right up man.

FRASER: (*Getting back to sussing out the possible rival.*) Giggles, do you write these stories for homework? Do the teachers tell you to write them?

GIGGLES: No. I just do it for something to do. We don't have a TV in my house.

SHOCK. The others have the same uncomprehending look of grief on their face as if they'd been told that the sun was going out. The mouths hang open. They don't know what to say.

FRASER: But…

PAUL: How can you…

ALAN: (*After a moment.*) Ha ha ha aha aha No TV!! No way!

PAUL: How come you've got no TV?

ALAN: 'Cause he's a special wee spastic. Ha ha ha ha ha

FRASER: Oh my God. Think of everything you've missed!

GIGGLES: I don't mind. I write stories.

FRASER: Stories? That's nothing man. How can you live without TV?

PAUL: It's the weirdest thing ever.

ALAN: Oh man, that's hefty. What a laugh. No TV. I'd hate to be you.

GIGGLES: My dad won't let me watch TV.

FRASER: What about your mum?

GIGGLES: I don't know.

A pause.

It's my birthday today.

EVERYONE: Oh. No way. Hefty. Happy Birthday. (*Etc.*)

FRASER: You never told anyone at school. We'd all sing if you'd have told us.

ALAN: What did you get?

GIGGLES: I'm nine now.

FRASER: So am I. I'm the oldest. Happy Birthday Gordon. Eh…

FRASER looks through his pockets. He has some change. He gives it to GIGGLES. GIGGLES is amazed but not smiling. PAUL follows this example and hands over about 20p in twos. ALAN does the same. There's no money in his pockets though. He pulls out a thick wedge of football stickers.

ALAN: I havenae any money. I spent it. I've got stickers though. You can have one.

FRASER: Wait! Have I seen those the day?

ALAN starts to flip through the stickers at an incredible pace.

Got got got got got got got got got got need got got got need got NEED!!!!!! Need man. When'd you get that?

ALAN: Ha ha ha. That's for you to know.

FRASER: Swap man. I've been after that for ages.

ALAN: Tough. Here Giggles you can have Paul McStay. I've got fifteen.

GIGGLES takes the sticker. Unsure of what it is.

GIGGLES: Thank you very much. Thanks Alan.

PAUL: Still no smile but. If you don't smile you cannae hang around with us.

FRASER: Aye he can. Giggles you can be our friend if you want. We all walk home together, but we stay on the cliffs for a wee while and look at stuff. You live in the flats don't you?

ALAN: Hey. I know something that will make you laugh. This is hefty man.

PAUL: What you gonna do Alan? That thing when you pull wee triangles of shite out your pants?

ALAN: No. That was a mistake.

FRASER: It is funny but.

ALAN: (*Huff.*) I'm no doing it now. Paul's ruined it.

PAUL: Just do it.

ALAN: Nut.

PAUL: Ach this is totally boring.

FRASER: (*Agreeing.*) I know. (*Pause.*) Tell us one of your stories Giggles.

ALAN: Naw!

FRASER: How no?

ALAN: 'Cause. It's stupid.

PAUL: You're stupid but we still hang about with you.

FRASER: Go Giggles. Tell us the story that won the competition.

GIGGLES: I don't mind telling stories. It's all right.

PAUL: Does it have any machines in it that talk and fight crime? They stories are hefty.

FRASER: Have you got it with you?

GIGGLES: I can remember it.

ALAN: This is a total neck.

The boys gather in a half circle, heading towards lying flat out.

FRASER: Go.

GIGGLES: This story is called 'The Garden In The Sky'.

ALAN: Neck.

PAUL: Shut your fat face you fat bas.

ALAN: You shut it.

PAUL: You shut it.

FRASER: Everybody shut it. Go Giggles.

GIGGLES: 'The Garden In The Sky'. Once upon a time…

GIGGLES leaps off the ramp. As he hits the stage below the lights change and there may be music. He addresses the audience directly in an adult tone. The others disappear from view and appear as the characters described below.

Once upon a time, in a land very far away there was an Emperor who was very, very rich.

FRASER appears at the top of the ramp as the emperor, wearing a gold crown.

He had a gold everything. Gold chairs, gold floors, gold walls, gold toilets. He even painted his servants gold and his dogs gold. Even though he was very rich, the Emperor was lonely. As he lay in his gold bed, with golden sheets, he couldn't sleep because he was so lonely.

FRASER mimes being very sad and lonely.

He asked his wizard what to do.

FRASER: Wizard, I'm lonely. Can you cast a spell to make it better?

Enter ALAN, beside him, wearing a wizard's hat.

ALAN: No problem Your Highness, I've got just the thing.

FRASER: It's not when you turn things gold is it?

ALAN: Sh sh sh, don't spoil this magic moment. (*In the style of a poor cabaret magician.*) Okay, I've got an ordinary stone here, have a feel at it, check it, make sure you're happy with it, it's a common or palace stone. Okay? Now I put it under this hanky…give it a minute… where you from…having a good time…I say the magic word… (*Suddenly Satanic.*) Ech bron dire tremeto wrath, don listin reeer! Coth realt vermerion la mer!!!!! (*Back to the lounge magician.*) And low and behold, what have we here but…

BOTH: A gold nugget.

ALAN: Thanks very much you've been a wonderful Emperor, goodnight.

GIGGLES: The Emperor was still very sad.

Exit ALAN. FRASER mimes seeing the girl as described below, keeping his eyes on GIGGLES.

One day, when the Emperor was looking out his golden window down to the town in the valley below his palace, he saw a young girl. The girl was picking flowers in the garden and singing a sad, sad tune. She had long black hair and rosy cheeks. She was the most beautiful girl the Emperor had ever seen. But what he liked best was that the girl wasn't wearing any gold at all. Just poor peasants clothes. The Emperor had never seen anyone without gold on. He asked his advisors,

Enter PAUL as an old advisor.

FRASER: Who is that sad girl in the garden?

PAUL: Why that is Kirsten, the butcher's daughter. She is poor. And she is sad. She hasn't smiled since her father killed her mother with his big butcher's knife.

FRASER: Why did he kill her mother?

GIGGLES: Asked the Emperor.

PAUL: He killed her because he is a mean, angry man and she was a happy woman who loved to sing and dance. The butcher thought she was witch. He cut off her head. Then he cut off her hands. Then the cut up her body and made them into sausages and ate them. He is very fat, this butcher.

Enter ALAN on ground level wearing a bloody butcher's apron. He mimes looking for his daughter – GIGGLES – and calling her in. He gets angry and exits.

FRASER: And very evil.

GIGGLES: Said the Emperor.

FRASER: From this day on, Kirsten will live in the palace as my wife and never see her evil Father ever again. She will be my Queen and she will be happy.

GIGGLES: And so they were married. The couple spent every minute together because they were in love. But it was soon the Queen's birthday and he didn't have a clue what to get her. He asked the Wizard. The Wizard said…

Enter ALAN as the wizard on the ramp.

ALAN: Get her a golden dog. Women love golden dogs.

GIGGLES: He asked the cook.

Enter PAUL wearing a chefs hat.

PAUL: Get her a golden pie. Women love golden pies.

Exit both.

GIGGLES: No good. The only thing the Emperor could think of was a golden bracelet. On her birthday he gave the queen the bracelet. The Emperor noticed how different she looked now. She didn't stand out as much in the golden palace. The servants were not as scared of her, because she was now golden, like them. He liked the way she was fitting in. So he bought her more gold. Golden crowns, golden shoes, golden rings and golden dresses. Soon she was all golden. She said 'But I am no longer the girl in the garden my husband'. He said…

FRASER: (*To GIGGLES.*) That is true. You are a queen now and shall dress in gold, as a queen should.

GIGGLES: One day the Queen was in the garden and stopped to pick flowers beside a lake. The weight of the gold dress she was wearing pulled her into the lake and under the water. (*GIGGLES struggles as if drowning.*) She tried to swim but her golden crown pulled her deeper and deeper and deeper until she drowned.

FRASER: NOOOOO!!!!!! (*He falls to the ground in grief.*)

GIGGLES: The Emperor ordered that the entire country was to mourn for sixteen years. He tore down all the gold in the country and threw it in the sea. When sixteen years had past he decided to build something to remember his beautiful wife by. He knew it could not be made of gold. So he decided to build a garden in the sky, full of the most beautiful flowers the world has ever seen.

ALAN enters with his wizard hat and a spell book. He stands beside FRASER.

ALAN: So we're all agreed on the Garden In The Sky spell? Last call for the Golden Dog In The Sky spell? (*A look from FRASER.*) Perhaps not. I say the magic word (*Again satanic chanting.*) Eech bach monair, zarh zarh ech ech gremant grontain, releet!!!! (*Normal.*) And there you go. (*Exit ALAN.*)

GIGGLES: The garden appeared above the town. It was a magnificent sight. Reds and blues and yellows and colours without names filled the sky. The Emperor smiled and said…

FRASER: If only I had left you in the garden my queen. If only…

GIGGLES: The people in the town were not happy. The butcher, who was an old man now was angry. He said…

Enter ALAN as the butcher on ground level.

ALAN: Kirsten was my daughter and the Emperor hid her away. They say she drowned but I know better. The Emperor killed her with a knife. He cut off her beautiful head and her beautiful hands. And now he builds a garden in the sky which the good people in the town cannot see because it is above our heads. Only those in the palace can see it. Let us destroy this garden, just as Kirsten would wish. (*He mimes the following.*)

GIGGLES: He went round the whole town, into the taverns and into the church. He gathered a crowd in the market place and had support from the mayor and the schools. The whole town stood below the garden and started to throw stones at the it. They screamed and shouted and enjoyed the havoc they were causing. Back in the palace the emperor saw what was happening and said...

FRASER: What do they want? Would they rather she was remembered with petals or with stones?

GIGGLES: Soon the townsfolk's stones had cracked the bottom of the garden. The butcher threw one last huge stone and the it broke. They gasped. They stared. The whole sky was suddenly filled with petals.

FRASER and PAUL throw petals over ALAN and GIGGLES.

The air was sweet and red and blue and yellow. The petals floated to ground and it was the most beautiful thing they had ever seen. Petals where there once was sky. The people cried with joy.

ALAN: It's the most beautiful thing I've ever seen!

GIGGLES: Said the butcher and he felt sorry for everything he had done in his life. The people danced as the petals floated around them. Never was a sky so brilliant. But very soon the petals hit the ground and there were no more to fall. The petals died on the hard pavements. The townsfolk looked sadly at the mess.

FRASER and PAUL sit down as children again. ALAN joins them exactly where they sat before.

No more beauty. No more petals to fall. They were sad and went home with heavy hearts. There was nothing left of the garden in the sky except a tiny seed which tumbled through a small crack in the pavement. Perhaps it will grow. Perhaps it won't.

Lights change back to the setting from before. GIGGLES makes his way back up the ramp to his position at the start of the story, a wee boy again.

The End.

The boys slowly come out of their story sleep.

FRASER: That was a big story.

PAUL: It was all right. A bit…babyish.

ALAN: The End? What happened? Did it grow? Aye. My wee brother Tommy reads stories like that. Ha ha ha.

FRASER: I liked it though.

PAUL: It was all right. You should write a story about a car that can speak though. A bit more our age.

ALAN: Or a car that can fly.

PAUL: Don't be a dick fatman.

ALAN: I'd better go. See yous the morra.

PAUL: We'll get you to the wee shop. Coming Fraser?

FRASER: Naw.

PAUL: Eh?

FRASER: I'm going to hang on for a wee minute. With Giggles.

ALAN: With *Giggles?*

PAUL: How come?

FRASER: Just.

PAUL: But we always walk home now.

FRASER: So? I'm hanging on, for a change.

ALAN: *We* can walk home Paul. You and me. If you want? For a change.

PAUL: I don't care. See yous later.

ALAN: (*As they exit.*) I'm no going to forget about that bet by the way. Not now not never. Tomorrow at school I'm going to keep talking about crackacookoos and soon everyone in the whole world...

ALAN and PAUL exit down the ramp, looking back every now and then. GIGGLES and FRASER awkwardly get to know each other.

FRASER: You live in the flats? I'm away up at the golf course. Paul lives in Miller Avenue. It's quite near you. His mum works in the Chemists and I don't know what his dad does. My mum and dad are both lawyers. What does your dad do?

GIGGLES: He's a ventriloquist.

FRASER: (*No idea.*) Aawwww right.

GIGGLES: He's got a puppet called Hugo. He's wooden and he loves Hugo more than me.

FRASER: What's it like?

GIGGLES: Horrible. Really, really horrible.

FRASER: Do you get to play with it?

GIGGLES: No. You're not allowed to play with it. It's my birthday today and Hugo and him do a show for me. It's my present. He says that people used to pay good money to see him and I should be grateful. I hate it.

FRASER: Do you hate your dad?

GIGGLES: I dunno. Do you?

FRASER: I think so.

GIGGLES: I hate Hugo. I know that for sure.

FRASER: Go and get him.

GIGGLES: Who?

FRASER: Thingby. Hugo. Go and get Hugo.

GIGGLES: It's not allowed.

FRASER: Who cares. If my dad had a puppet I'd steal it.

GIGGLES: Would you? What would we do with it?

FRASER: Em…eh…I know. There's the wee school. It's ace and it's haunted. That would be hefty.

GIGGLES: A haunted school?

FRASER: Hefty.

GIGGLES: What'll we do when we get there?

FRASER: I dunno. Stuff.

GIGGLES: (*Thinks about it.*) Right. I'll get him.

FRASER: Hurry up.

GIGGLES runs off. Black out. Spot up on FRASER and PAUL running across the stage. They are nineteen. PAUL has long hair, down to his neck. FRASER's hair is attempting to do the same but not really carrying it off. They are both wearing the same 'Wonderstuff' T-shirt. PAUL is wearing long shorts. FRASER sports ripped jeans. The politics of the three boys has levelled out. FRASER is no longer the leader. He and PAUL are on an equal footing. They're also a bit drunk and laughing.

Quick! Up to the rocks!!!

They exit at high speed, stage left ground. Laughing all the way. They enter up the cliff, collapsing.

(*Looking back.*) Oh no way man.

PAUL: Serves him right.

FRASER: Do you think they caught him?

PAUL: Fat bastard. Serves him right.

They laugh and sit.

Who was that that started chasing us?

FRASER: Dunno, some guy. I don't know why Alan went down Shanty Shaws. He's bound to get caught. Here, before Alan gets here. Guess who I got off with last night?

PAUL: Alan's mum.

FRASER: Tina. I couldnae believe it. Down the beach. Alan was about ten metres away.

PAUL: She was steaming though.

FRASER: Obviously. When was the last time you got off with someone and both parties were sober?

PAUL: It's not an option.

FRASER: Exactly. You should see university mate. Girls drink like fishes. Cider and black, Southern Comfort, Yards of Ale…wait a minute. How did you know she was drunk?

PAUL: She told me. I shagged her this afternoon.

FRASER: …?

PAUL: So? You've shagged her.

FRASER: Aye a year ago! She's engaged to Alan.

PAUL: She was going out with Alan a year ago.

FRASER: Aye but they're engaged now.

PAUL: Ach they've been going out since they were fourteen. They either had to get engaged or split up. Anyway you were just boasting about getting off with her.

FRASER: I wasn't boasting, I was confessing.

PAUL: Same difference. She's nice Tina. She's clever. And funny. She can do so much better than Alan. She wants to split up but doesn't have the guts. They're like an old married couple. Ach I dunno. Work tomorrow.

FRASER: Me too.

PAUL: *What?* You work at the putting green mate. That's not work. You just sit in there listening to tapes and pretending to read books.

FRASER: It's ace. As soon as it rains we pack the whole thing up and go to the boozer.

PAUL: And they wonder why no tourists come here any more. Lucky nimstons. I have to hump bloody great boxes all over the place. And it doesnae stop at the end of summer.

FRASER: You should definitely go to Uni. It's ace.

PAUL: Nah.

FRASER: It's amazing. Meeting all different folk. It opens your awareness and…and creativity…juices…know what I mean? You cannae work in a factory all your life.

PAUL: (*Confused.*) I'm no gonna am I? The band. The only reason I'm working at Kelco is to get enough money for a van. Once we get signed… Boom.

FRASER: Once we get signed – boom.

PAUL: I can't wait until we get signed man.

FRASER: I lie in bed worrying about it. We'll be the first famous people to ever come from Girvan.

PAUL: And we're not coming back. What we going to do about Giggles?

FRASER: Awww. Just tell him straight out. He's mad. He just stays in all day doing nothing and writing these hor- rible…things. And his ideas for the band…man. He's mental. Have you seen this? (*Pulls out a lyric sheet and reads.*) This one's called 'The Black Hole Of Feminism'. I mean, Christ how do you write a chorus around that? Morrissey couldnae even do that.

PAUL: Between you and me mate, I can't stand Giggles. We need to tell him that he's out the band.

FRASER: God. It's all he thinks about though. He says that it's his way out.

PAUL: It's our way out too. I hate the wee fanny. I always have. We have to do it. For the good of the band.

FRASER: A lot of folk have said he's good on stage. At our last gig at the 13th Note some wee guy said he looked like Ian Curtis.

PAUL: Aye, because of the slash marks on his wrists. Anyway he's not to the same music. We're into The Stuffies and The Beatles and The Smiths and bands like that. And he's into all these...mad...mental American guys I've never even heard of.

FRASER: Alan's into heavy metal and he's still in the band.

PAUL: Alan's the drummer though. He doesn't have any musical input. You're the singer, you should tell Giggles.

FRASER: You're the guitarist.

PAUL: You outrank me. He's just an extra. He's like a manic depressive Bez. Only not as funny. He's got to go.

Enter ALAN (19) up the ramp. Drunker than the other two. He has long greasy hair and a Whitesnake T-shirt. He collapses next to the others.

FRASER: What happened?

PAUL: Did you get caught?

ALAN: Gentlemen, I am now a fugitive from the law. I'm an outlaw. I'm a crack troop of commandos jailed for a crime they did not commit.

FRASER: What happened?

ALAN: Well seeing as I was abandoned by my so called friends I had to make a run for it by myself. Somebody must have seen us doing The Garden Run and gave chase. Well it turns out the police were sitting waiting in Henrietta Street...

PAUL: What do you mean 'waiting in Henrietta Street'? Are you trying to say this was an elaborate sting operation?

ALAN: I'm not saying anything. All I know is the pigs came after me and left yous.

FRASER: The pigs! He's been on the run for two minutes and he's already picked up the jailhouse vernacular.

ALAN: The rozzers, the filth, the screws, the boys in blue. All of them came after me. So I bombed it down to Shanty Shaws and hid. They were shining their lights in going 'it's no good hiding, we can see you'. But they couldn't see me. Oh no, nice try boys, but I'm trained. I'm a man of action. I remembered everything I'd learned in the BB's and for all intents and purposes became…invisible. Crouching, blending, watching, waiting. My senses were alive, my instincts burning, my eyes were like that. (*Opens eyes wide and looks side to side.*) It was like 'Nam all over again. I was ready. If they made the slightest error, the merest lapse, I would be gone, breezing past them, into the night.

PAUL: And did you?

ALAN: Did I what?

PAUL: Did you breeze past them into the night?

ALAN: Nah, they fucked off after about a minute. One of them needed a dump.

FRASER: Ha ha ha. Man of action!

ALAN: Well at least I didn't run away.

FRASER: Yes you did! That's what we were doing, we were running away. All of us.

ALAN: Chickens.

PAUL: Just because you were running slower than us doesn't make you any braver.

ALAN: Chickens.

FRASER: Okay, okay when you go back to Tina tonight you can tell her that you were a big hero.

ALAN: Oh I will. Hey Tina told me about you, by the way.

FRASER: ...what?

ALAN: You. Mr Lonely Heart.

FRASER: What you talking about?

ALAN: Tina said that last night you were totally steaming and you tried to get off with her. She said no and you started greeting saying you were dead lonely at University and that you really fancied her.

FRASER: I am...*appalled.*

ALAN: So am I. Greeting and everything. Sad. It's all right, I know tons of people fancy her. Paul's fancied her since second year.

PAUL: I shag her all the time when you're not there though, that's the difference.

ALAN: Ha ha ha, you wish.

PAUL: No I do.

ALAN: Yeah. (*To FRASER.*) Never mind mate. You'll fall in love one day.

FRASER: I am appalled. Alan, I never said anything like that to Tina. I'm not lonely at University. At least I'm in Halls and not living at home and travelling everyday. How can you be a student living at home?

ALAN: I don't care. I like it here. Too many memories.

PAUL: Aye all bad.

ALAN: Naw. For instance, it was on this very hill that I coined the word Nimston. And now everyone calls everyone else a Nimston.

FRASER: Only us lot.

PAUL: Was it you that came up with Nimston?

ALAN: Yup. It was the day Giggles told his first story. The first of many. Oh by the way I met him just there and told him he's out the band.

PAUL & FRASER: *What?*

ALAN: I just met Giggles there and I told him he was out the band.

Pause.

What? That's what you wanted wasn't it?

PAUL: Aye but…

FRASER: What did you say? How did you phrase it?

ALAN: I said, 'Giggles mate, you're ripping our stitches with all this crazy crap you do. You're out the band…'

FRASER: Oh my…

ALAN: I said 'It doesn't mean that you can't hang around with us or anything. You just can't come to the practices or write any lyrics.'

FRASER: Oh my God.

PAUL: How did he take it? Did he have one of his attacks?

ALAN: Naw. He was fine. He said he was joining another band anyway and going away on tour. He had a guitar case with him. He knew already.

FRASER: How did he know already?

ALAN: (*Shrugs.*) Says he expected it what with everything else. I think he's back to his 'Police File' stuff again.

PAUL: Uh oh.

FRASER: His what?

PAUL: Ach, during the winter there, when you were away, Giggles got obsessed with 'The Police File' in The Carrick Gazette. You know the bit in the paper where they tell you crimes of the week. 'Man caught urinating on dog' and everything...

FRASER: Aye.

PAUL: He said the only way to be remembered in this town was to get in the Police File. He got quite excited by it. We didn't see him for weeks. Turned out he's been caught setting fire to the police station.

FRASER: No way. Did it get in the paper?

PAUL: Nut. They were so embarrassed that a wee guy had broken in and poured petrol about the place they kept it quiet.

FRASER: How come no one told me this before?

ALAN: So I think he's up to his old tricks. Said it was time to go to the wee school.

PAUL: The wee school?

FRASER: What makes you think he's back to The Police File stuff again?

ALAN: 'Cause he said 'I'm gonna get in The Police File if it kills me, and tonight's the night'. I thought to myself, 'Aaaahhaaaa.'

PAUL: Dick.

FRASER: Do you think he's going to set fire to the wee school?

PAUL: The wee school? Why would he do that?

FRASER gets up and exits without saying a word to anyone. PAUL and ALAN exchange a glance.

ALAN: I'm no going man. He's pished his bed and now he's got to sleep in it. I'm a fugitive from the law.

There's a warrant out for me. More or less. If he's setting fire to stuff he's on his own.

They walk off down the hill slowly. No one is listening to ALAN babbling on. Suddenly there's a terrific explosion off stage and a red glow throbs over the lighting. They are thrown back in shock. A quick glance at each other and then they exit at high speed, shouting.

End Of Act One.

ACT TWO

The stage is exactly the same as we left it. The ramp, some chairs and the tarpaulin covered thing in the corner. FRASER (19) is sitting on the edge of the ramp looking out to sea. He is wearing a crumpled shirt with a loose floral tie. He sighs. ALAN (19) appears at the bottom of the ramp wearing a smart shirt with a black tie and holding a paper plate piled high with sausage rolls. He creeps up behind FRASER trying to hold in laughter. He gets right up behind him and grabs him by the shoulders.

ALAN: Aaargh!!! Saved your life!!! Ha ha ha ha!!

FRASER screams until he realises it's just ALAN. Then he flakes.

FRASER: Jesus fucking Christ Alan!!! Christ sake man!

ALAN: Ha ha ha you shat yourself.

FRASER: (*Genuinely furious.*) You're such arsehole! What were you doing? What were you doing?

ALAN: All right calm down man.

FRASER: Naw I'll no calm down. You're an idiot. You could have killed me!

ALAN: No way.

FRASER: I…I mean…after what…you shouldnae do that.

ALAN: I'm sorry. Jesus Christ.

FRASER: You never think man. You just…you're such a…

ALAN: I'm sorry. Sorry. (*ALAN sits next to FRASER, who is still annoyed.*) Sausage roll?

FRASER: No.

ALAN: They're nice.

FRASER: NO.

ALAN: I brought them for you. I'll not eat them.

FRASER gives ALAN a look to say that he's firm on the sausage roll issue. ALAN shrugs and starts to eat them. After a pause which would be awkward if ALAN was aware of that type of thing.

Do you think seagulls like sausage rolls? Mind you they eat anything don't they? Seagulls? Don't they?

FRASER: What are you doing?

ALAN: Eh?

FRASER: What are you doing?

ALAN: (*Confused and holding out the plate.*) I...

FRASER: Why aren't you back at the hall?

ALAN: Oh right. I was looking for you.

FRASER: Why?

ALAN: Dunno. I saw you run off. Thought you might want some company. And to a lesser extent some sausage rolls, ha ha.

FRASER: Well I don't.

Pause.

ALAN: (*Not taking the hint.*) It was a nice funeral.

FRASER: It wasn't a funeral.

ALAN: Aye I know, but it was a nice service.

FRASER: It can't be a funeral if the guy's not dead.

ALAN: Well...everyone seems to think he's dead.

FRASER: I don't. Do you? Honestly?

ALAN: Aye.

FRASER: Honestly?

ALAN: Aye.

FRASER: You don't exactly seem upset about it.

ALAN: I am.

FRASER: You don't look it.

ALAN: So?

Another shorter pause.

FRASER: When was the last time you saw him?

ALAN: In the street that night.

FRASER: Right. And did he look suicidal?

ALAN: No more than usual. He's always had a bit of that though, 'member when he slashed himself.

FRASER: Aye only cos that guy in the NME did it.

ALAN: So?

FRASER: So when was the last time you saw someone in the NME burn down a school? And did he say he was going to burn down the school before or after you chucked him out the band.

ALAN: It wasn't just me that chucked him out the band. You wanted him out in all.

FRASER: Aye but...

ALAN: And he never actually said he was going to burn down the school anyway.

FRASER: But don't you think it's convenient that he comes up here the minute we go down there and yet we never bumped into him. And he leaves his clothes and that guitar case full of his wee stories all ready to be found. It's whatdoyoucallit, Reggie Perrin. I just don't think he'd do it

ALAN: I think he would. I think he would. It's a shame for him.

FRASER: All I'm saying is it'd be more like him to jump out later and say 'ha ha ha, you're all a bunch of nimstons, I win, you loose!' and I think I knew him better than anyone.

ALAN: Well. I dunno. It was a good turn out. Just shows you.

FRASER: Just shows you that people in this dump are a bunch of gossipy, nosy, self righteous idiots looking for something to do.

Enter PAUL (19) up the ramp again wearing a black tie. Looking and feeling quite solemn.

PAUL: All right my man?

ALAN: All right mate, how you doing?

PAUL: No bad. What yous doing up here? The party's started.

FRASER: Party.

PAUL: Well you know the thingby, the reception in the hall.

ALAN: Sausage roll?

PAUL: No ta. I'm sausage rolled out my nut.

FRASER: Who was that you were talking to?

PAUL: Giggles' auntie. She's from Glasgow.

FRASER: What she say?

PAUL: Nothing.

FRASER: Well you were talking to her for ages.

PAUL: I don't know, just stuff. I don't think she knew Gordon very well.

FRASER: Gordon?

PAUL: What?

FRASER: You're calling him Gordon now?

PAUL: Well...

ALAN: What did you make of the songs they played in the church? The Cure? No way. I didn't even know he liked The Cure.

FRASER: He didn't.

PAUL: Aye he did.

FRASER: Since when?

PAUL: Well, I remember him saying one night in The Swee. You weren't there. I didn't know what else to say when they asked. I said that and The Beatles cos, you know, you can't go wrong with The Beatles.

FRASER: They asked you? Who?

PAUL: The minister an' that. I thought they'd asked you as well.

FRASER: Naw.

PAUL: Listen they were saying it might be an idea for the band to play later on. Just a couple of songs maybe some of the ones Giggles wrote?

ALAN: I'll need to go up the road to get the kit.

PAUL: Okay boss. I thought we could chuck in a couple of covers, if they want, just so it doesn't get too depressing.

FRASER: What?

ALAN: *Losing My Religion.* Always a favourite.

PAUL: It's just a couple of songs mate. To remember Giggles.

FRASER: No. I'm not doing it. I don't want to play in the band. Ever. I...I'm leaving. I'm leaving the band.

PAUL: (*Laughing. Not taking this seriously.*) Fuck sake.

FRASER: We're no doing anything anyway. I'm too busy at Uni. And I'm thinking about doing my own stuff, getting a fourtrack, acoustic gigs and that.

PAUL: When you going back?

FRASER: My dad's driving me up tonight.

PAUL: Well you can do the gig first. Do you want to take some of the stories with you?

FRASER: Naw. I'm away. Now. See you later right.

PAUL & ALAN: See you.

FRASER exits away down the ramp.

PAUL: Pfft! The band's no breaking up. No way. Here, there's a PA in there already. They use it for Bingo. Are you going to get the kit?

ALAN: Might as well. (*Goes to leave.*) Listen…can I get one of those stories?

PAUL: How?

ALAN: I dunno. Just to kind of…I dunno.

PAUL: It's probably better if we keep them together. Just in case.

ALAN: Oh aye right. (*Pause.*) It's funny Giggles leaving the stories isn't it? They're good. 'Member the one about all the birds who stopped flying?

PAUL: (*No.*) Aye.

ALAN: Aye. They are good. We should sell them and make a bomb. Ha ha.

PAUL: Go and get the kit.

ALAN: (*Sarcastically.*) Yes Sir! (*Turns to leave.*)

PAUL: Don't bring the gong.

ALAN: (*Disappointed.*) Eh? How no?

PAUL: Just.

ALAN: If Fraser's leaving the band right enough we should get Tina in to sing.

PAUL: He's no leaving the band.

ALAN: Aye but if he does, it's an idea. Think about it. I'll be back.

PAUL: Okay.

ALAN leaves PAUL alone on the ramp. Lights down on PAUL wondering about what lies after the band. A beat. Lights up. GIGGLES (9) appears lying flat on the ramp. He lowers himself down to ground level with great difficulty and looks around, terrified. There's a 'Psst!' noise from the ramp. It's FRASER (9). He too is lying flat on the ramp. FRASER hands a large ventriloquist's dummy down to GIGGLES. GIGGLES sits it on the floor and then helps FRASER down to the ground. They are climbing into the wee school via a broken window.

FRASER: See…I…told you…this was…(*Thinks he sees something, screams in fear.*) HEFTY!!!!

GIGGLES: Aaaaaahhhhhhh!!!!!

FRASER: Aaaaaahhhhhhh!!!!!

GIGGLES: (*Not moving.*) Run!

FRASER: No wait. Wait. It's chairs. It's tiny wee chairs. I thought it was a ghost but it's chairs. Ha ha ha ha. This is a good laugh isn't it?

GIGGLES: (*Obviously not laughing.*) Aye.

FRASER: It's all right this actually. Bet Alan and Paul have never been in here. It was my big cousin that invented it. The police caught them and brought my big cousin back in the police car. It was in the Police File in the paper. This is hefty.

GIGGLES: How do we know the ghosts aren't here already? Watching us?

They both look round slowly.

FRASER: (*Unsure.*) Naw.

They look around again.

Naw. Maybe it isnae haunted.

GIGGLES: It is.

FRASER: How?

GIGGLES: I can feel it. I know it's haunted.

FRASER: (*Getting the fear.*) Shut up. You don't feel ghosts.

GIGGLES: You do. You can tell that there's something going on in here.

FRASER: Shut up.

GIGGLES: Something scary.

FRASER: Shut your face Giggles. Anyway I'm not scared.

GIGGLES: He used to be famous.

FRASER: Who?

GIGGLES: Him. (*Sits Hugo on the floor in the middle of the room.*)

FRASER: Him?? How come?

GIGGLES: He used to be on TV. He was on this programme and it was on live right...

FRASER: Right.

GIGGLES: And my dad was going to be really famous right...

FRASER: Right.

GIGGLES: But Hugo wouldnae work. He was broke or something. And everybody saw him not working. That's how I'm not allowed a TV. In case it's on again. I hate him. He works now. In the house. But he doesnae work if other folk are watching so it's only me that gets to see Hugo speaking.

FRASER: Get him to say something now. Get him to say tons of swear words.

GIGGLES: You do it. I can't do it.

FRASER reluctantly picks up Hugo and puts his hand inside.

FRASER: (*Shakes it.*) It's no working.

GIGGLES: Pull the string inside and his mouth moves. Then you speak.

He does.

FRASER: Ace. 'My name is…eh…'

GIGGLES: Hugo.

FRASER: 'Hugo. And I'm a…fucking bastard. BAS-TARD!!' Hee hee hee, I'm good at this by the way. (*Throws Hugo to the ground.*) Coming we'll smash something up?

GIGGLES: What?

FRASER: I don't know. Something. I think we should.

GIGGLES: I think we shouldn't.

FRASER: How?

GIGGLES: Ghosts.

FRASER is beginning to get the fear.

FRASER: (*Looks round.*) I thought you said you had to be in soon for your tea?

GIGGLES: No. He won't care.

FRASER: Giggles, I don't think we should tell anyone about us coming here.

GIGGLES: How not?

FRASER: We might get into bad trouble. The police might get us and we'll go in the paper. My mum and dad would flake. They don't let me do anything. I get shouted at if I do anything. They'd be sorry if I die.

GIGGLES: Fraser? See if I die? Gonna wait until I come back as a ghost? Don't be scared though. I'll be a good ghost and we can be friends.

FRASER: All right. See if I die? Gonna tell everyone that I fought the ghosts off with a stick and I was punching and kicking and jumping off of stuff and blood was going everywhere and I was totally winning but I could see that they were all battering you so I totally flew over and started to save you but it wasnae really you it was a ghost trick and they came at me from all sides and they got me. Right?

GIGGLES: Right.

FRASER: (*Picking up Hugo and doing a voice.*) 'Hello there. I said hello there!'

GIGGLES: (*Turning, frightened.*) Hello Hugo.

FRASER: 'And what's your name Giggles?'

GIGGLES: Gordon.

FRASER: 'Gordon. That's a nice name. Where do you come from?'

GIGGLES: Here.

FRASER: 'What here in the wee school?' Ha ha ha. (*Pause.*) 'You're not allowed in here you bad boy. He's never going to get anywhere with this attitude is he? Are you?'

GIGGLES: No.

FRASER: (*Getting vicious.*) 'No. You're never going to get anywhere. You're going to fail at everything unless you sharpen up boy!'

GIGGLES: Shut up.

FRASER: 'Sharpen up! I've never failed at anything. When I was your age I was head boy. I'm a winner and you're a loser. And you'll always be a loser unless you sharpen up your ideas!!!'

GIGGLES snaps and leaps on FRASER and Hugo. There's a lot of screaming and punching from GIG-GLES. They are all on the floor. FRASER rolls away and we see that it is Hugo being attacked. GIGGLES is out of control and is spitting and crying and scream-ing and punching. FRASER takes a second and then leaps on Hugo helping GIGGLES smash the dummy to pieces. GIGGLES is screaming...

GIGGLES: I'm going to kill you! I'm going to kill you! I'm going to kill you!!!! (*Etc.*)

FRASER: (*Looking stage left in a panic.*) There's someone coming! There's someone coming!!!

They use a chair to climb out the way they came grab-bing the remains of Hugo as they go. Noises off stage left. Enter ALAN (29). He is moving quickly. He goes to the machine covered in tarpaulin in the corner. Without removing the sheet he checks to make sure that everything is in order. He looks excited and happy. He checks to see if the others are coming. No sign of them yet. A moment passes. He remembers. He looks very fragile now. Sad and young. His head drops. But he's used to this feeling and must have some way of snapping out of it, because in a second he's shrugged that darkness off of himself and he's okay again. He sees PAUL (29) and FRASER (29) entering stage left.

ALAN: Come into the parlour.

FRASER: (*Looking about.*) Holy Christ. It's exactly the same.

PAUL: It's a bit parky mate. Is there no heaters or any-thing?

FRASER: It's exactly the same! They re-built it to look exactly the same. Nothing's changed at all

ALAN: (*Awkward.*) Heaters?...eh... Hang on. (*ALAN exits stage left.*)

FRASER: Paul this is mad. I can't do this. I can't cope man.

PAUL: There's nothing wrong. It's okay.

FRASER: (*About ALAN.*) I don't think he knows what he's doing. He's acting like he's organising a barbecue or something.

PAUL: Ach it's just his way. He's trying his best.

FRASER: (*Seeing the machine.*) And what do you think *that* is?

PAUL: Well...I don't want to spoil the surprise, but I think it's a heater.

FRASER: A heater?

PAUL: He builds heaters in his hut. Tina says he's been out in his hut for about a month building this. She says that he comes up with heaters and radiators and stuff but modifies them, then re-names them. Like he's invented it again you know? He calls them Viking names. Tina says that she's got a radiator, a leaf blower and a sewage pipe named after her.

FRASER: How romantic. And when did she tell you all this?

PAUL: We stay in touch.

FRASER: (*Shaking his head.*) Unbelievable. You're standing there giving it the old best mates routine with Alan and all these years you've been shagging his wife?

PAUL: It's complicated boss. You don't know anything about it.

FRASER: Oh don't I? You're not denying it though?

PAUL: It's complicated. It's not been all the time. It kicked off again when they were in London. I'm in love with her. It's as easy as that.

FRASER: What about him?

PAUL: I'm his friend. Some people suit this life. Tina doesn't. I don't know what I'm doing really.

FRASER: Jesus Christ.

Enter ALAN.

ALAN: Couldn't see any heaters Paul mate. I've a feeling that it'll heat up later.

PAUL and FRASER look at the covered machine and then to each other.

Seats! (*He grabs three seats from wherever they are and sets them up centre stage. They are children's seats and they all sit very uncomfortably.*)

PAUL: Well… Let's start. As you know it's been ten years now. A lot's happened since then. The reason we're here is to remember Gordon Temple. Giggles. Em… perhaps it'd be better if I told you a bit about what I've been doing? When they found that guitar case full of the stories down at the Horse Rocks as you know there was that letter which said they belonged to the three of us. Somehow the whole lot ended up at my house. I'd look at them every now and then and say to myself, 'I should do something with these'. Anyway, about that time I got a job in London. Just labouring with my uncle, but the girl I was with was an art student and she did wee paintings for the stories as part of her course work. She printed them up in her college and left them in libraries and schools and stuff. No money of course, but we *had* made some connections. One day we were at a book fair thing in a library in Clapham and I got talking to this woman who ran a wee publishing house. I won't bore you with the complications, but I ended up seeing her and getting a nice wee job in her office. Every time we'd do a kids book or fairy tales, I'd slip in one of Giggles' stories, see if we'd get a bite. A couple got taken up here and there and when the money came in I'd split it three ways. You'd notice it wasnae much. Then about three months ago, I got a call from a very famous American publisher who wanted to use 'The Garden In The Sky', 'The Tide Pool' and 'The Bird's Strangest Decision' in a collection of short stories with a view to an international deal. It looks like Giggles' stuff will finally get an audience. Big bucks. So we thought this would be a good time to get together, have a chat and maybe read a few of the stories and then go our separate ways.

ALAN: Hear hear. About the stories not the separate ways. Well it's been all go for me lately what with the...

FRASER: Wait a minute.

PAUL: What?

FRASER: Have we all got to do a wee speech? Like Alcoholics Anonymous?

PAUL: We need to catch up.

FRASER: Do we? To what end? I mean, if I understand this correctly, this little meeting is to remember Giggles and for you to tell us that the stories are getting published. Why do we need to do a speech?

ALAN: I also have some news and a machine.

FRASER: Okay. But do we need a speech?

PAUL: What harm can it do? Go ahead amigo.

ALAN: Righto. As I say it's been all go lately with the 2000 development project. The outreach teams have finally got their arse in gear and we're seeing results. The golf course roundabout is basically a sweetener though. I'm hired as consultant by the client to design and oversee the building of the strategy plans and the physical construction of the landscaping. I was part of Scottish Enterprise's bubble group in rechannelling community strategies and I led the work group tutorial refocusing team who came up with the seven stage plan to fresh line the high end actuality numbers. Add to that my routine on site and you can see that it's a living nightmare most of the time.

PAUL: Mmmm. Sounds like you're kept busy.

ALAN: Oh I have to. I'm always busy. I like to be busy.

PAUL: So anything else?

ALAN: Let me see…we bought the house when we got married. I work. Ach there's been loads of things here and there that have happened, but I can't remember them now. Tina's fine. She says hi. Em, Dad died about two years ago. Tommy came back from the states for that. Aye, it was sad.

PAUL: Sorry I couldn't get back for that Alan.

ALAN: We appreciated the card Paul. Thoughtful.

PAUL: Fraser.

FRASER: What?

PAUL: What you been up to?

FRASER: Nothing.

PAUL: Must be something.

FRASER shakes his head.

Well… Something'll turn up. The money'll be coming in for the stories soon.

FRASER: I don't want money from the stories. I don't even want to think about the stories. We're probably not even due any money from them anyway, if he's still alive.

ALAN: Oh come on.

PAUL: Let's not start all that.

FRASER: I realise that would shatter your little publishing empire and the goal of your life Paul, but I happen to think it's something worth considering. I've said that all along. Everyone's just taken the easy way out.

ALAN: I can get you a job if you want Fraser. It'll no be much but it'll be steady. You could come back home.

FRASER: (*Shakes his head.*) Jesus Christ.

Pause.

ALAN: Maybe em… (*Glances at the machine.*) No, maybe not. Or maybe we should read out one of the stories? Eh? Read us one of Giggles' stories, Paul.

PAUL: Will I? Which one?

ALAN: Em…what about the…

FRASER: Read the one about the magnets.

PAUL: The Bad Magnet? How do you know about that one?

FRASER: I've read it. I've read all of them.

PAUL: Okay mate. Good choice. Let's see, where is it? Here we go. (*Jokey.*) Are you sitting comfortably?

ALAN: No.

FRASER: Just fucking read it.

PAUL: Then I'll begin. In a time of Atomic clocks…

Story state. They clear the stage and GIGGLES appears, addressing the audience directly as before.

GIGGLES: In a time of Atomic Clocks. When people stopped believing, when people stopped looking, all The Things stopped working. People were angry at The Things.

Enter FRASER.

FRASER: Hey Things!

GIGGLES: They said.

FRASER: We made you. We created you. What right have you got to stop working?

GIGGLES: The Things stayed very quiet about the whole business. They were, after all, just Things. The people, being after all, just people, thought that they could get by without any Things at all. They were wrong. After a short while without The Things, the people died out.

FRASER collapses and is dragged off by ALAN and PAUL.

It was a time of shouting and blame. A time of confusion and anger. But it was also a very interesting time to live in and there were laughs to be had, so most of the people didn't mind too much. People, it seemed, were no more. It was time that The Things took over.

Enter FRASER, ALAN and PAUL marching in unison.

Things are very different from people. They tend to just get on with their business. They tend to keep themselves to themselves. On the whole they have a quiet life, uninterested in other Things. There are of course exceptions. Fireworks for instance. (*FRASER mimes a firework.*) And bullets. (*PAUL mimes a bullet.*) And paint. (*ALAN mimes paint.*) These Things are noisy and eager to be noticed. They poke their noses (if you can say that Things have noses) into other Things. But on the whole Things are solid, reliable, likeable and happy. Better than people in almost every way. Soon though, The Things got restless. They got bored. And in no time at all most Things wanted more in their lives. They wanted to be like The People.

They mime the following.

The Things formed a government. They had TV shows. They watched other Things playing sports. They fell in love and got married. They went to work and complained about other Things. It was a good life for The Things. That is, it was a good life for all The Things except The Magnets.

They become magnets.

The Magnets had been as happy as all the other Things when the people left but now they were very sad. You see a magnet *needs* other Things.

FRASER is walking along smiling when ALAN leaps out and sticks to him, knocking him over.

But this really annoyed The Things.

FRASER: Stop sticking to me Magnet. Stop pulling me Magnet. Stop attracting me Magnet. We can't get on with our lives with you holding us back like this. Go away!

GIGGLES: They said. And so The Magnets went away.

The three of them move away up to the back of the stage.

They moved to a small town near the sea, where they knew they wouldn't annoy the big, important Things. They thought they would be happy living with each other, falling in love and getting married and doing the stuff that Things were always going on about.

They mime out the following.

But no. You see when two Magnets come together, instead of attracting each other, they push each other away. And no matter how deeply the Magnets were in love, they could never cuddle, they could never kiss, because the closer they came the further they were repelled. The whole town was in a panic. They couldn't stick together at all. As they walked down the street they were repelled. When they played in the parks they were repelled. When they worked or danced or moved towards each other, they were repelled. In short, they could not be together. The Head Magnet called all the Magnets as close as they could come.

PAUL: My brothers and sisters. We are all Magnets. Known for the ability to attract and bring together Things. It is with a tear in my eye and a stone in my soul that I say this; we cannot live together. It's a scientific fact. We are destined to never be with another Magnet. We are to wander the Earth, lonely and sad. We will try not to bother the Things as they go about their business. But don't be too desolate my friends. Remember the good times. Remember that we brought Things together. We held Things firm. We were once important. We pulled Things towards us.

GIGGLES: All the Magnets were very sad. One in particular. He was sad because he had fallen in love with a beautiful Magnet he had seen from a distance. He had tried to get close to her, but of course he had been pushed away. He thought, 'The only way I could get close to her is to become a bad Magnet. If I was a bad Magnet, I wouldn't pull things towards me, and I wouldn't be pushed away.' He had heard that the only way to become a bad Magnet was to be hit very hard until your powers stopped. Obviously another Magnet couldn't do this, so he had to do it himself. (*GIGGLES runs up the ramp to the edge of the cliff.*) He went to a high cliff, took a deep breath, and threw himself off. As he fell he smiled to himself. (*Shouts.*) 'I'm a bad Magnet and soon I'll be close again!!!!!'

GIGGLES leaps off the edge into a blackout. Lights up again on the whole stage. PAUL (29) is pacing up and down excitedly. ALAN (29) is tinkering with the machine. FRASER (29) sits as slumped as he can be in the tiny chairs. FRASER is losing patience. Some time has passed between the end of the story and now.

PAUL: I'm not exaggerating. I think Giggles will be remembered as an original genius. Probably the first this area's produced since Burns. And if you think about it, what is this, if not a version of a Burns Night? Getting together, reading his work, remembering his life and having a good time...

ALAN: Nearly there.

PAUL: His stories have the same universal appeal as Burns. I think with the right support Giggles could be a major figure in literature. And his life…so short, so brutal. It's all there. I find it amazing that he could have produced all this top class work in such a short space of time and buried under that deep, black personality.

FRASER: Paul. Stop.

PAUL: What mate?

FRASER: Stop it.

PAUL: What?

ALAN: Nearly there…

FRASER: Paul. You've read these stories a million times right? It could even be said that you've based a good bit of your life on them. Does nothing strike you as strange at all?

PAUL: (*Hard.*) What do you mean?

FRASER: The stories. These wonderful stories that get you so excited and make all your money. Are you telling me that they've never seemed odd to you?

PAUL: Why should they be odd?

FRASER: Why should they be…? The first story we heard, if memory serves, was 'The Garden in The Sky', right? He was nine. *Nine.* Could a nine year old boy write that story? Of course not, it's ludicrous. He started at nine, he stopped at nineteen, and in those ten years he wrote a guitarcase full of stories; all in the same voice, all in the same tone and structure. They have an allegorical style that is way beyond a nine year old boy. Christ half of them are parables!

ALAN turns round to follow this argument.

PAUL: I agree it would be ludicrous if we were talking about a normal nine year old boy, but Giggles was obviously an original genius.

FRASER: Are we talking about the same person here? Giggles was a strange, twisted, poor wee soul who just couldn't get on with folk. We couldn't stand him most of the time and when we weren't ripping the piss out of him we were running away from him. I don't think it's realistic to assume that this wee boy could produce work of this standard.

PAUL: (*Getting very angry.*) So what is realistic then Fraser? I'm interested. You're obviously an expert on this so fire in.

FRASER: Maybe he copied them from somewhere. Maybe his dad wrote them I don't know.

PAUL: No you don't know. First off, I spend all day everyday with writers and publishers from all around the world. If he'd copied them from somewhere, believe me, I'd know. Secondly, his dad? I don't think so. If you remember, his dad was an insane alcky who sat slumped in that flat all day stinking of pish who only ever got up to batter Giggles. That's why Giggles was a storyteller. He was a dreamer, he *had* to be. It was genius by necessity. That's why he poured himself into those stories!

FRASER: No that's why he was fucking miserable! That's what you don't understand. That's what no one at the service understood. He wasn't a troubled teenager or an adolescent depressive. He was *always* like that. From day one. He was born miserable and there was nothing we could do about it.

PAUL: Yes there was. We could've listened to his stories…

FRASER: Oh come on.

PAUL: We could've listened to him instead of mocking him.

FRASER: We were children!!!! How could we…

PAUL: We could have treated him better…

FRASER: I did. Compared to you. You always hated him and talked about him and everything and suddenly he did his vanishing act you're acting like his biggest fan, just in case he's watching from somewhere.

PAUL: It wasn't a vanishing act Fraser, he fucking drowned.

FRASER: How do you know? How can you be sure?

ALAN: Right lads settle down.

PAUL: Giggles left behind stories and he left them to us. Why would he do that if he was still alive? I happen to think it's our duty to do something to make sure he's not forgotten. And now you're giving it the old 'Oh I don't think he really wrote them'. 'I don't think he's even dead!' Well who cares? It doesn't matter man.

FRASER: You never saw him write the stories.

PAUL: It doesn't matter ya moron!!! You've always got to drag everyone down with you haven't you? It's always someone else's fault.

FRASER: At least I'm not a hypocrite.

PAUL: I'm not a hypocrite. I know what I am.

FRASER: I know what you are too. Say one thing do another, you've always been like that.

ALAN: Settle down, c'mon.

FRASER: Settle down? What you talking about? This is why we came here isn't it? So we can get this over with.

PAUL: We're here to remember Giggles.

FRASER: Well we don't seem to be making a very good job of it do we? You remember him as a poet genius struggling with demons, Alan remembers him as an old mate who can't be with us and I remember him as a manic depressive whose life was made a misery by an abusive father, he couldn't handle it, so he's done a fucking bunk.

PAUL: He killed himself. He killed himself because his stories were going unread, his genius was being snuffed out by the town and the...the...

FRASER: Shit.

PAUL: He killed...

FRASER: You're talking rubbish...

ALAN: Please, c'mon.

PAUL: Shut up! You're just taking the easy way out. You're ignoring the facts, you're just ripping away all ties.

FRASER: Don't tell me about how I feel about anything. You don't have a clue.

PAUL: At least I'm living life, not just giving up and moping about. And I'll bet you blame it all on Giggles. I'll bet you love telling your mates about 'this horrible thing in my past man, it affected me man. I could never face things after that.' I'll bet they think you're dead deep for being a wanderer and a loner and all that bollocks. Cop out! Giggles wrote those stories all right. That's why he killed himself.

FRASER: (*Flaking.*) He killed himself because the fucking band was splitting up ya dick! The band. It had nothing to do with his stories. He had these teenage ideas about getting famous in the band, fat boy here told him that we were going to chuck him out so he set fire to a building and jumped off a cliff. Easy as that.

PAUL: Nah.

FRASER: Aye. A stupid, adolescent, band going nowhere. Do you think if he really thought so much of the stories he'd dream about the band all the time? Nah. *We* knew it wasn't forever. Giggles didn't. So instead of teaching the town a lesson by getting famous, he taught the town a lesson by setting fire to something. He didn't care about the stories and neither should we.

PAUL: Nah.

Pause. As usual, the people doing all the shouting feel stupid and shaky. The anger is still floating around.

ALAN: Did I tell yous that Tina's pregnant?

They look at him but can't find the words to speak.

Came as a bit of a shocker I can tell you. I'd been away at a battle re-enactment thing. I'd been helping out some of the English Civil war mob down in the black country somewhere. Their organisation was an absolute disgrace. Really it was a fiasco. Most folk didn't even know what side they were on and the kit was just bits of cardboard and Halloween costumes. Anyway, I was meant to be away all weekend but I just headed home Saturday night. I got home to find Tina lying on the bed, greeting her face off. Just crying and crying and crying. She wouldn't say what the hell was wrong. My heart was beating man, I tell you. I thought she'd got cancer or something. She eventually told me she was up the duff. Well I said that's good news! We can afford it, we've got room, good job, we're happy and everything. She...she said she didn't want my baby. She loves me and everything, she just doesn't want my baby. (*Pause.*) Dr McCulloch says it happens all the time. Chemicals released into the body and everything. It's difficult. I've to give her room. So I'm in the hut most nights building stuff and thinking about things. She'll come around. Hope.

Pause. FRASER is staring at PAUL with an evil smile.

FRASER: Tell him.

PAUL: Shut up.

FRASER: Tell him.

PAUL: Shut up.

ALAN: Tell me what?

PAUL: Nothing. He's an arsehole.

ALAN: No tell me.

FRASER: I think you should. Prove to me that you're not the hypocrite I think you are. It would help.

ALAN: (*Serious.*) What's he on about mate? You got something you want to tell me?

A stare out. It looks very like ALAN already knows about PAUL and Tina and is challenging PAUL to admit it. Long silence.

PAUL: He...he wants me to say that I think Giggles copied the stories.

ALAN still holds PAUL's eye. He lets it go.

ALAN: Right. Mind you they said the same about Shakespeare didn't they? Who knows, maybe Giggles was a genius? I think I'd like that.

FRASER: Oh well.

PAUL: (*To FRASER.*) You're a sad man. A sad, sad man.

FRASER: Yeah.

PAUL: I actually think you're jealous.

FRASER: Jealous? Jealous of who?

PAUL: Of Giggles. Of the memory. He'll be remembered. You won't.

FRASER: I've got news for you *boss*, Giggles won't be remembered. It's time you realised Paul that no one's going to remember we were even here.

PAUL: I think you should take that advice then and piss off.

FRASER: I'm going.

PAUL: Good.

FRASER: Don't bother sending me any more cheques, I don't want them.

PAUL: Good.

FRASER: Goodnight.

PAUL: Goodnight.

FRASER: Good luck with the baby Alan. (*FRASER gets as far as the door.*)

ALAN: Wait! I haven't told you my news.

FRASER: Yes you have. Congratulations.

ALAN: No not that. My word news.

FRASER: What 'word news'.

ALAN: Feels daft. Me telling you this now. Maybe you should just go.

FRASER: Oh just tell me.

ALAN: Well… Remember that first afternoon on the hill? When Giggles told us about 'The Garden In The Sky'? Do you remember the bet?

FRASER: The bet?

ALAN: We made a bet to see who could get a word into the dictionary.

FRASER: No.

ALAN: (*Embarrassed.*) I've done it. I mean there's a word of mine in a dictionary. Not the real dictionary. It's a civil engineering handbook. Scottish Enterprise decided they needed a dictionary of new business terms. I was in charge of the headline group who chose the words. I remembered the bet and thought it would be a nice thing if I put in a word. Nimston. My word was Nimston. It means an area specifically kept clear for the workers to keep their stuff. So it's in there. Alongside the real words. It doesn't matter now.

FRASER: Not really. A nice thought though. But it doesn't matter. I hardly think Nimston is going to become a world renowned phrase.

ALAN: (*Shakes head.*) You are a dick Fraser. I can't be bothered any more.

PAUL: Just go, man.

FRASER: Why? So you can be alone with your best pal?

ALAN: I'm going home.

FRASER: Aye, go home. Home to your loving wife's arms. Home to your hut. Where you build all your heaters and radiators and pretend that you're happy. We know that you've built a heater that you think will really impress us. It's a fair bet that it's called the Giggleatron or something. Bet you think we'd be all moved at this wonderful gesture. Let's have a look at it. (*He whips off the tarpaulin and there is indeed a machine underneath which looks like a generator or something.*) Oh it's a…what is it? Furnace perhaps? A heater? Could it be?

PAUL: Shut up man.

FRASER: No. Alan's went to a lot of trouble. How do you switch it on Alan? Eh?

ALAN: Don't switch it on. Not now.

FRASER: But you've went to all that effort! No we must see this beast in action. Let me see…

ALAN: Don't. Please. Fraser.

> *FRASER pushes a starter button. ALAN looks at the floor ashamed. PAUL is drawn closer with curiosity. A shudder, a grunt, a whirl. The machine comes alive. They all look about the room for a clue to what it does. Then it starts. Slowly at first. Gently… Petals begin to fall from the roof. More and more petals of soft colours. Reds, pinks and blues. They fill the air, they cover the men, they float and swim over the set. A gust… Petals fall all over the theatre. All we can see are flowers. GIGGLES appears on the ramp.*

GIGGLES: The air was sweet and red and blue and yellow. The petals floated to ground and it was the most beautiful thing they had ever seen. Petals where there once was sky. The people cried with joy. The people danced as the petals floated around them. Never was a sky so brilliant. But very soon the petals hit the ground and there were no more to fall. All that remained of the Garden In The Sky was a tiny seed which tumbled down, into a crack in the pavement...

When all the petals have fallen, we can see that ALAN, FRASER and PAUL are gone and the stage is empty.

The End.

9 781840 022445